KAṆḌARIYĀ MAHĀDEVA TEMPLE OF KHAJURĀHO

KAṆḌARIYĀ MAHĀDEVA TEMPLE OF KHAJURĀHO

K. M. SURESH

BHARATIYA KALA PRAKASHAN
DELHI (INDIA)

Published by :
C.P. Gautam
Bharatiya Kala Prakashan
3611/5, Narang Colony,
Tri Nagar, Delhi - 110035
Ph. : 7192770

First Published : 1999/ 2015/2018

ISBN : 81-86050-08-6

Typesetting by :
Brij Mohan Gupta
4615/13, Tri Nagar, Delhi-35
Ph. : 7108270

Printed at :
Santosh Offset,
40, Anand Nagar,
Delhi-110 035

Dedicated to

Loving Memory of

My Revered Brother-in-law

Shri C.T.M. Kotraiah and

My sister Smt. T.M. Sulochana

of Chilugod Village.

CONTENTS

FOREWORD

Khajurāho, a modern village situated on the left bank of Khudra-Nala, a tributary of the Ken river, in the district Chhattarpur of Madhya Pradesh was one of the capitals of Chandellas, but it is better known for a group of temples, built between the 9th and 12th century A.D. The Chandella rulers were devotees of both Śiva and Viṣṇu. In their inscriptions, Śiva is invoked as Mahādeva, Viśvanātha, Maheśvara Kedara and so on; their well known Śiva temples are the Mataṅgeśvara, Viśvanātha and Kaṇḍariyā Mahādeva.

Of these, the Kaṇḍariyā Mahādeva temple is the finest largest and the loftiest of temples at Khajurāho. This was built during the reign of Vidyādhara, between c. 1025 and 1050 A.D. It measures about 30.5 mts. in length and height and 20 mts. in width, excluding the platform; it rests on the fully developed *jagati* and consists of *mukhamaṇḍapa, maṇḍapa, mahamaṇḍapa* with lateral transepts; *antarāla* and *garbhagṛha* enclosed by an inner ambulatory passage with transepts on the side and on the rear, while its elevation consists of *jagati* (platform), *adhiṣṭhāna* (bansement), *jaṅghā* (wall portion) and *śikhara*.

This temple displays a large number of sculptures of arresting beauty. They appear on the three bands of its walls and represent gods and goddesses, *mithuna* and *surāsundarīs, vyālas* and *nagis*. This is the only temple which displays who *makaratoraṇas*.

All the components of the temples have their roofs, each higher than the other, and each with a cluster of peaks around the central nucleus. The roof over *mukhamaṇḍapa, maṇḍapa* and *mahamaṇḍapa* are of pyramidal *piḍhas* and the highest roof over the *garbhagṛha,* culminates in a tall *śikhara* to which are clustered four *ura-śriṅgas* on each side, including *karṇa-śriṅgas* and *naṣṭa-śriṅgas,* constituting minor peaks of smaller sizes, producing a remarkable effect.

Though several books on Khajurāho monuments and sculptures have been published, this author has his own justification to publish yet another. He aims at presenting a detailed and systematic account of Kaṇḍariyā Mahādeva temple, studying its sculptures and iconography with the help of the *Āgamas, Purāṇas* and other texts.

Dr. Suresh is a studious scholar and has done an intensive study of the sculptures and iconography of this temple. His documentation is thorough, and his explanation appearing. I am sure the art historians will welcome this as a work of serious scholarship.

15th August, 1998

Prof. S. Settar
Chairman
Indian Council of Historical Research
New Delhi

PREFACE

Indeed, I was thrilled by the magnificent temple of Kaṇḍariyā Mahādeva and its sculptures in and around this temple, which was built by the Chandella ruler Vidyādhara between Cairca 1025-50 A.D. This is one of the finest, largest and loftiest temple among the group of temples of Khajurāho. This temple mark the culmination of the Central Indian building style and fully developed in the saptaratha on plan and in elevation which marks the highest development of Hindu architectural design.

In this monograph, the Chapter I and II deal with location and general history of Chandellas. The Chapter III deals in details with general description and architecture of the Kaṇḍariyā Mahādeva temple. The Chapter IV deals with the sculptural art, iconography, social life and society as depicted in the sculptures, erotic sculptures and surāsundarīs.

A few books on Khajurāho monuments and sculptures comprehensive study of particular temple with its sculptures and iconography. This work aims at presenting a detailed and systematic study of temple and sculptures in particular.

I am grateful to Professor S. Settar, Chairman, Indian Council of Historical Research, New-Delhi, for contributing a foreword to this monograph and for his kind words of appreciation. My grateful thanks to Shri C.T.M. Kotraiah who gave encouragement and took immense pains in guiding me at every stage this work.

I acknowledge sincerely the help given by Shri A.K. Sinha and Dr. Narayana Vyas, Bhopal Circle of Archaeological Survey of India, as usually providing good photographs of monument and sculpture. I am thankful to the staff of Khajurāho Museum. My thanks are also due to my wife Smt. Gauri Suresh, who, throughout the process of this work, was a source of inspiration to me.

I will not forget my debit to Shri C.P. Gautam of Bharatiya Kala Prakashan, Delhi, for his kind co-operation and quick printing this book.

4-3-1998
Kamalapaur-583 221

DR. K.M. SURESH
Director (Museum)
Kannada University, Hampi
Vidyaranya Campus

LIST OF PLAN AND PLATES

Chapter-I

GENERAL INFORMATION

Khajurāho (Lat. 24°-51' North and Long. 79°-56' East) is a modern village, situated on the left bank of Khudrā nālā, a tributary to the Ken river, in the Chhatarapur District of Madhya Pradesh in Central India. It is situated 65 kms. south of Mahobā, 47 kms. east of Chattarapur, 44 kms. north-west of Panna, 175 kms. north of Jhānṣi, 400 kms. south of Bhopāl, the capital of Madhya Pradesh and is linked to these places by good metalled roads as well as nearest rail connection to Harpālpur and Satna being 102 kms. and 117 kms. There is also a daily air service linking Khajurāho with New Delhi-Agra and Vārāṇasī. Khajurāho has a number of Five-Star as well as good number of economy hotels, tourist bungalow dormitories and huts maintained by Madhya Pradesh Tourism and Special Area Development Authority, where the tourists can stay comfortably. There is also a Circuit House available for occupation with the permission of Collector, Chattarapur and Sub-Divisional Officer, Khajurāho.

The Kaṇḍariyā Mahādeva temple remains open to the public from sunrise to sunset with nominal entry fee of 50 paise per visitor for monuments and Archaeological Museum, maintained by the Archaeological Survey of India.

Chapter-II

LEGENDS AND HISTORY

Khajurāho is known as Kharjjūravāhaka in the inscriptional records[1] and according to traditions, this place was so called because one of its city gates was ornamented with two golden Khajūr trees. The literary works like Pṛthvīrājarāsö of Chand Bardāi[2] mentions that Khajurāho is called Khajurāpura or Khajjīniapūra. According to Abu-Rahim[3] who accompanied Sultān Mohmed of Ghazanī, mentions it as Khajurāhā and Ibūn-l-āthir[4] mentions Khajurāho as the territory of king Bida, Vidyādhara. Ibn-Battūtā, who visited this place in 1335 A.D., calls this place as Kajarrā or Kajra[5] in his graphic description of this place and monuments.

The track round the Khajurāho was known during the ancient times as Vaṭṣa, in the medieval times as Jējākabhukti and from the 14th, centuries onwards as Bundelkhaṇḍa, the track of land that lies to the south of Jumna and north of Vindhyās, east of the Betwā river and west of the river Tamasā. Bundelkhaṇḍa is now a part of Viṇdhya Pradesh, formed by union of Bāghelkhaṇḍa and Bundelkhaṇḍa with a total area of 24,600 square miles which is situated between Uttar Pradesh and Madhya Pradesh[6].

The land of the Chandellas was known in the Chandella epigraphic and later contemporary records as Jējābhukti[7], Jējābhuktika[8] or Jējākabhukti[9], the ancient name of modern Bundelkhaṇḍa. The boundaries of the Chandella dominion varies from time to time, but it always included Mahobā, Kālañjar, Khajurāho and Ajayagaḍh, all of which are situated in the central segment of Bundelkhaṇḍa. According to Khajurājo inscription[10], the extent of the Chandella kingdom was marked by the towns of Bhāsvar on the river Mālavā on the west, the Jumna on the north with Gopādri or Gwālior in the north-east and the Kaimūr hills on the Narmadā river on the southern frontier. The area indicated approximately coincides with the modern Bundelkhaṇḍa.

History

The tradition says that the original home of the Chandellas was at Māniyagarh, a hill fort, about 19 kms. south of Khajurāho, in Chattarapur District. The Chandella dynasty rose to power during the early 10th century A.D., and survived as a powerful independent royal family until the close of the 13th century A.D. Before coming to the power, they were feudatories under the Imperial Pratihāras. The decline of the Imperial Pratihāras, gave golden opportunity to Harṣa and Yaśovarman to establish their sovereignty over the Central India by capturing the important forts of Kāliñjara[11] and Chiṭṭakūra. The period of transition and political re-adjustment which had always intervened between the fall of one imperial power and the raise of another in India had already begun.[12]

The Chandellas ruled for a period of over three centuries from 10th to the beginning of the 14th century A.D., whom after a protracted resistance, they were finally overwhelmed by the invasions of the Muslims. Thus the Chandellas were among the last defenders of Hindu rule against the onslaught of the Muslims. A fragmentary Mahobā inscription[13] giving

GENEALOGYA OF THE CHANDELLA DYNASTY

Nānuka (c. 831 A.D.)
Vākapati

Jayaśakti (c. 850 A.D.) — Vijayaśaki
Rāhila
Harśaa (Kañcuka)
Yaśovarman (Pūpapa)
(c. 925 A.D.)

Dhaṅga (c. 950-1003 A.D.) — Kṛṣnappa (Aśarva)
Gaṇḍaa (c. 1003-1018 A.D.) — Devalabdhi
Vidhyādharaa (c. 1018-1022 A.D.)
Vijayīpāla (aBhauvanadevi)
(c. 1022-1051 A.D.)

Dëvavarmana (c. 1051 A.D.) — Kīrtivarmana
(c. 1070-1098 A.D.)

Sallakaśaṇavarmana (c. 100 A.D.) — Prithvīvarmana (c. i125 A.D.)

Jayāvarmana (c. 1117 A.D.) — Pratāpa
Madanavarmana - Valhanadëvi
(c. 1129-63 A.D.) - Lakhamadëvi
Caandaladëvi
Yaśovarmana II (c. 1165 A.D.)
Paramārdi (c. 1166-1202 A.D.)
Trailokyavarmana (c. 1205-1247 A.D.)
Vīravarmana (Kalyānadëvi) (c. 1247-86 A.D.)
Hammīravarmana (c. 1289-1308 A.D.)

Chandella royal genealogy upto Kīrttivarman (Circa A.D. 1060 to 1100) states that Jējābhukti was named after king Jēja, just as the *Pṛthvī,* the earth, was designated after king Pṛthu.

Harṣa

Among the earlier rulers of Chandella, Harṣa was a notable prince, who succeeded Rāhila, and made a steady progress towards the attainment of a significant status in the political history of North India. He reinstated his over lord Kṣitipāla or Mahipāla of Pratihāra, on the throne of Kanauj in Circa 917 A.D.[14], which was shaken by the invasions of the Rāṣṭrakūṭas of the Deccan. This achievement was probably commemorted by him by the construction of the Mātaṅgeśvara temple, which was the earliest sand stone temple to be constructed at Khajurāho. The allusion to this important political incident in the Khajurāho records is a clear indication of the growing power of the Chandellas as a independent power force from political subservience to the imperial Pratihāras.

Yaśovarman

Yaśovarman alias Lakṣavarman, the son of Harṣa succeeded to the throne and laid the foundations of the greatness. He won back the fort of Kālañjara in Circa 940 A.D., from the Rāṣṭrakūṭas, which had been earlier wrested by them from the Pratihāras. The occupation of Kālañjara fort was a significant achievement of Yaśovarman and destined to figure prominentely in the later history of Chandella dynasty. According to Khajurāho inscription[15] of his son Dhaṅga dated 954 A.D., Yaśovarman built a magnificent temple dedicated to Viṣṇu in the form of Vaikuṇṭhanātha, which is identifiable with the Lakṣmaṇa or Vaikuṇṭhanātha temple at Khajurāho.

Dhaṅga

Dhaṅga son of Yaśovarman, succeeded to the throne and ruled from Circa 950 - 1002 A.D., he boldly discarded the tutelage of the Pratihāras, consolidated the Chandella kingdom, by extending his territories and made it the strongest power of North India. He was not only a great king and conqueror but also greater as a patron of art and architecture. The temples of Viśvanātha and Pārśvanātha are the two finest surviving monuments of Khajurāho. The Viśvanātha temple was built by the king himself and the Pārśvanātha temple was probably built by one Pāhila, who was honoured by the king Dhaṅga.

Gaṇḍa

Gaṇḍason of Dhaṅga, succeeded to the throne, had a very short period Circa 1002-1004 A.D.,[16] but peaceful region of his paternal domension. His region is known from only a few later inscriptions, one from Mahobā[17] and another from Maū[18]. It is evident from the inscriptions that he was able to preserve his territory without being too much aggressive like his father and grandfather. The Vaiṣṇava temple, now known as Jagadaṁbī and the Sūrya temple called as Chitragupta temple, may be attributed to this king although there is no direct evidence.

Vidyādhara

Gaṇḍa was succeeded by his son Vidyādhara to the throne and ruled from Circa 1004-1029 A.D. He was a most powerful ruler and won victories over the Kalachūris and Pratihāras[19]. He is recognised by the Muslim Chronicler Ibn-n-l-Āthir[20], as Bīda and described him the most powerful ruler of his time.

He organised an active resistance against Muslim invader, Mahmūd of Ghazanī, twice in 1019 A.D. and 1022 A.D., when the latter invested the fort of Kālañjara. He was a great patron of art and built a highest and finest temple known as the Kaṇḍariyā Mahādeva temple, which is one of the most splended Chandella temple at Khajurāho. The inscription[21] on a maṇḍapa pilaster, mentioning a king called viriṃda appears to be the another name of Vidyādhara, who is known to the contemporary Muslim Chronicler as Bīda.

Vijayapāla

Vijayapāla ascended to the throne after the death of Vidyādhara in 1029 A.D. But after the death of Vidyādhara, virtually the Chandella power began gradually to decline owing largely due to the determined onslaughts of Kalachūris and Muslim invaders. The later Chandella rulers were ineffective and Paramārdin was the last ruler whose reign was ended with his defeat at the hands of Qutbuddīn Aiback in Circa 1202 A.D. The Chandella power did not recover from the shock of this defeat and slowly faded out of the stage of history. The later Chandella rulers concentrated on the hill forts of Mahobā, Ajayagaḍh and Kālañjara for strategic reasons.

References

1. E.I., Vol.I, p.147, verse, 63.
2. *Pṛthvīrājarāso* Ed.by. S.S. Dās & M.P. Paṇḍit, p.2.
3. *Alberuni's India,* Trans, by. E.Sachan, Vol.I, p.202, London, 14.; *The Rehla of Ibūn Battūta.,* Ed.by. Mahdi Hussain, Gaikwad's Oriental Series CXXII, Baroda, 1953, p.166.
4. *Ibūn-l-Āthir, Al-Tarikh-ul-Kamīl,* Bulek, 1874, IX, pp.115-116.
5. *ASR,* Vol.II, p.412.
6. *Hindustan Year Book,* 1952.
7. *E.I.,* Vol.I, p.122.

8. Ray, H.C., *Dynastic History of Northern India,* Vol.II, p.1212, Calcutta, 1936, & *E.I.*, Vol.I, p.35, verse 10.
9. *ASR,* Vol.XXI, pp.173-174.
10. *E.I.*, Vol.I, p.122, line 6.
11. *Ibid.*, Vol.I, p.122.
12. Ray, H.C., *Op.cit.*, Vol.II, p.1212, Calcutta, 1936.
13. *E.I.*, Vol.I, p.221, line 6.
14. *Ibid.*, Vol.I, p.122, line 10.
15. *Ibid.*, Vol.I, pp.123-35.
16. *Indian Archaeology*—A Review, 1971-72, p.55, line 22.
17. *E.I.*, Vol.I, pp.217-218.
18. *Ibid.*, Vol.I, pp.195-207.
19. *Ibid.*, Vol.I, p.219 verse 22.
20. *Ibun-l-Athir, Al-Tarikh-ul-Kamil,* Bulek, Vol.IX, pp.115-116.
21. *ASR,* Vol.XXI, p.62, Krishna Deva, *Temples of Khajurāho,* Vol. I, pp.370-371.

Chapter-III

ARCHITECTURE

General Description

The contribution of Chandella rulers in the field of art and architecture are highly significant. They are traditionally reputed as great builders and enthusiastic patrons of art and architecture, which is confirmed by the magnificent group of temples at Khajurāho, which was a religious capital and the most important centre of their kingdom. According to *Paramāl Rāsō*[1], the Chandella rulers constructed as many as 85 temples at Khajurāho, but only 25 temples now stands in varying stages of preservation.

The temples of Khajurāho mark the culmination of the Central Indian building style and reveal certain distinctive peculiarities on plan and elevation. They are compact, lofty, without any enclouser wall and stands on a high platform the *jagatī,* which elevates the temples from its environs and provides an open air promenade and ambulatory around the temple. All the compartments of the temple are interconnected internally as well as externally and are planned in one axis running east to west having *ardhamaṇḍapa, maṇḍapa, aṇtarāla* and *garbhagṛha.* In a larger temple, *maṇḍapa,* turning into a *mahāmaṇḍapa* and introduced inner ambulatory around *garbhagṛha* which is added another pair of lateral transept and a rear transept, each with a balconied window for the ventilation of the interior. Some of the large temples have a subsidiary shrine reared up in each of the four corner of the *jagatī* rendering the structure a complete *pañchāyatana.*

The temples errected on a lofty platform, the *jagatī,* has an emphatically high *adhiṣṭhāna*, over which rests the *jaṅghā* forming central zone consisting of solid walls alternating with voids of the inner compartments. Above the *jaṅghā* rises the roof consist of a series of graded peaks that virtibly resemble a mountain range. The roof over the compartments rises in a modulated crescent from the lowest over the *mukhamaṇḍapa* to the loftiest over the *garbhagṛha.* The roof over the *mukhamaṇḍapa, maṇḍapa* and *śikhara* over the *garbhagṛha* is a tall and curvilinear in design of *rekha* type with a lyrical outline. The clustering together of subsidiary *śikharas* to the main one not only lightens the weight of stupendous pile but also accentuates the soaring effect of the main *śikhara.*

The sanctum of developed temples of Khajurāho are in *saptaratha* on plan and in elevation and the cubical portion below the *śikhara* divided into *saptāṅga bāda.* The *saptaratha* sanctum with *saptāṅga bāda* of Khajurāho temples marks the highest development of Indian architectural design.

THE KAṆḌARIYĀ MAHĀDEVA TEMPLE

The Kaṇḍariyā Mahādeva temple is one of the finest, largest and loftiest temples of Khajurāho and is dedicated to Śiva in the form of Śiva-Liṅga enshrined in the sanctum-sanctorum. This temple measures about 30.5 mtrs. in length and height and 20 mtrs. in width excluding platform. The temple rests on a high platform, the *jagatī* and consists of a plan the *mukhamaṇḍapa, maṇḍapa, mahāmaṇḍapa* with lateral transepts, *antarāla* and *garbhagṛha* enclosed by an ambulatory with transepts on the sides and on the rear. (Plate No.1) Its mature plan and design, grand dimensions and symmetrical proportions, superb sculptural embellishment and architectural elaboration, all mark it out as the most evolved and finished achievement of the Central Indian building style and one of the sublime creations of Indian architecture. Further, this temple presents each constitutent element of the plan and elevation on a grand scale and with considerable elaboration of design and ornamentation. It has an extensively indented plan with the largest number of projections and recesses which are rhythmically carried up on the elevation.

This temple displays largest number of sculptures of alluring beauty appears on the three bands on its walls and represented gods and goddesses, mithunas, apsarās, surasundaris, vyālas and nāgis in recesses. This is the only temple which displays two *markaratoraṇas.* As this temple is striking similar to the Viśvanātha temple and was completed in Circa 1002 A.D., it is slightly later than Viśvanātha and may plausibly be assigned to Circa 1025-50 A.D. Support is lent to this suggestion by the find of a short epigraph on a *maṇḍapa* pilaster of this temple, mentions of a king called Virimda, which may have been a pet name of Vidyādhara[2].

The temple consists on plan and has *mukhamaṇḍapa, maṇḍapa, mahāmaṇḍapa* with lateral transept, *antarāla* and *garbhagṛha* (Plan No.1) enclosed by an circumbulatory with transepts on the sides and on the rear and on elevation (Plān No.2 and 3) consists of *jagatī* (platform); *adhiṣṭhāna* (basement); *jaṅghā* (wall portion) and *śikhara* over the *garbhagṛha.*

Jagatī

The temple rests on a fairly extensive 10 feet high *jagatī* (the platform). The original facade of the *jagatī* seems to have survived only a bit towards south-eastern corner, on the flank of the imposing flight of steps leading to its terrace. The mouldings consist of *bhītta* decorated with lotus petals, *jāḍya-kuṃbha* and *paṭṭīkā*.

Adhiṣṭhāna

The temple stands on a high *adhiṣṭhāna* which is errected on a fairly extensive and high *jagatī*. The mouldings of the *adhiṣṭhāna* consists of *pīṭha, jādakuṃbha, karṇīkā, grāssapaṭṭa, kapōta, khūra, madhya-bandha, kuṃbha, kalaśa, antarapaṭṭa, gagaraka, kapōta* and *vasantapaṭṭīkā*. The *antarapatī* decorated with processional frieze representing horse and elephants, warriors and hunters, dancers and devotees, acrobats and musicians and miscellaneous scenes including erotic themes. The niches on the *adhiṣṭhāna* displaying images of *Saptamātrikās* with Gaṇeśa and Vīrabhadra.

Jaṅghā

The *jaṅghā,* the wall portion of the temple has three rows of sculptues of equal size demarcated by two series of mouldings. The mouldings consist of a projecting grassapaṭṭikā, stencilled scrolls and row of sculptures, that is, gods and goddesses, Vidhyādharas, Mithunas and erotic scenes.

Śikhara

The varāndika mouldings separating the *jaṅghā* from the *śikhara* comprise a pair of *kapōtas* intervened by a broad recess. Above the *varāṅdika* rises the roof and all the compartments of temple have their own roofs, each higher than the other and each with a cluster of peaks around the central nuclear. The roof over the *mukhamaṇḍapa, maṇḍapa* and *mahāmaṇḍapa* are of domical pyramidal type of *pīḍha* and roof over the *garbhagṛha* is of *rekha* type of *śikhara*. The roof over the *mukhamaṇḍapa* is of pyramidal one in a small scale. The row of sculptured niches is surmounted by a pediment and is flanked on each side by a model pyramidal rooflet. The crowning member of the roof occurs a *kūṭaghaṇṭā* comprising two *pīḍhas, candrikā, āmalaka, kalaśa* and *vijayapūraka*. The roof over the *maṇḍada* is also pyramidal one with little bigger than *mukhamaṇḍapa*, having all the features.

The roof over the *mukhamaṇḍapa* is also a model of pyramidal one with bigger in size with all the components. The *pañcaratha* plan of the *mahāmaṇḍapa* is reflected in the rooflets and the four rooflets forming the basal horizontal row, two on each side of the central bunch of pediments crowning the sculptured niches. Over these rises a pyramid of four of other horizontal rows of rooflets. These are symmetrically arranged in vertical as well as horizontal rows and have a marked diagonal progression converging the crown of the *mahāmaṇḍapa*.

The roof over the *garbhagṛha* culminates tallest *śikhara* (Plate No.2 & 3) to which are clustered four *ūrah-śriṅgas* on each side, besides numerous *anga-śikharas* constituting minor peaks of smaller sizes. The *śikhara* is *saptaratha* variety comprising *rath, naṇḍīka, pratiratha* and *karṇa*. The main *śikhara* is of twelve *bhūmis* indicated by eleven *bhūmi-āmalakas* of semi-circular section. All the *rathas* of the *śikhara* project beyond the shoulder and the crowning members of the *mūlamañjarī* above the *grīvā* comprise *āmalaśarka*, three *candrikās*, smaller *āmalaka, candrikā, kalaśa* and *vijayapūraka*. All the other *śriṅgas* are of a uniform size and flanking the main *ratha*. To fill the voids between the attached *śriṅgas* a few *naśtā-śriṅgas* of graded highest have been inserted at various levels, producing a rythmical effect. The *śikhara* is covered with a mesh of *caitya* arch filled with sculptures.

The temple on plan has *mukhamaṇḍapa, maṇḍapa, mahāmaṇḍapa, antarāla* and *garbhagṛha* (Plan No.1). The temple is entered through *mukhamaṇḍapa, maṇḍapa, mahāmaṇḍapa* with lateral transept, *antarāla* and *garbhagṛha.* At the main entrance of the temple is provided with an elegantly carved *makaratōraṇa* of four loops (Plate No.4). The upper edges of the loops are decorated with *kīrttimukha* and a running frieze of dancers and musicians while within the loops depicted Vidhyādhara couples. The outer face on the flanks of *makaras* depicting two figures of Śiva-Pārvatī and the inner face with Lakṣmī-Nārāyaṇa on the right and Brahmā and Brahmāṇī on the left side respectively.

Mukhamaṇḍapa

The *mukhamaṇḍapa* has four pillars of square section with cardinal projections, decorated on the upper one-third with stencilled scrolls and pot and foliage, carrying a square capital which supports kumāra brackets. The beam is surmounted by a cornice with three ornate offsets decorated with gōgarkās, triangular frills and lotus petals. Above the cornice rests a square ceiling of the *nābhiccanda* order composed of five cusped flowers of three tiers of kolas each. The central one is deeper than the remaining.

Maṇḍapa

The *maṇḍapa* has eight pillars and four pilasters which

are similar to those of *mukhamaṇḍapa.* A pair of inner pillars has an abacus depicted with a divine couple above the kumāra brackets. The cornice has broad offset on two sides decorated with lotuses in relief on the soffit. The cornice also reduces its length and converts it from a rectanguler to a square. The square is then turned into a circle by cutting the corners which are carved with *kīrttimukhas* and scrolls. The inner ceiling has a circular design of eight flowers of each two tiers with a large void in the centre representing the seedpod of a flower design. This is the only temple which has another *makaratōraṇa* at the entrance to the *mahāmaṇḍapa.*

Mahāmaṇḍapa

The *mahāmaṇḍpa* of this temple was a variation from a simple rectangular plan, which is peculiar to this temple, which reflects the outer plan and provides additional thickness for *mahāmaṇḍpa* are of square in section with cardinal projections and rests on a heavy base with the usual mouldings. The upper section carriers capital of usual design surmounted by eight other kumara brackets, the corner ones being smaller in size. The bellies of the upper kumāras are piereced with sockets for the reception of apsarās and vyāla struts. Only two apsarās are survived in these sockets in the *mahāmaṇḍapa* of the temple, one each on the south-western and north-eastern corner pillars.

The upper brackets carry a beam decorated with stencilled scrolls, grāsapaṭṭikā and a frieze of gandharvas and Vidyādhara couples carrying garlands and playing on musical instruments. The beam is surmounted by a cornice of the usual design. The ceiling comprises five concentric circular flowers with a central bud, the seed pod. The *kīrttmukhas* in the corners are pierced by sockets for apsarās, of which three figures are survived. The transept has two pairs of pilasters with usual type of base, decorated shaft, capital and brackets. The interspace between the pilasters shows two apsarās, standing on lotus leaves. The balconied openings has two pillars and pilasters. The cornice supports a plan and flat ceiling.

Antarāla

The pillars of the *antarāla* have shaft of octagonal, sixteen sided and circular sections resting on a heavy octagonal base with the usual mouldings. The pillars of the *antarāla* flanking the *garbhagṛha* doorway and the doorjambs depicted with Śaiva *dvārapālakas* and female *Cauri* bearers.

Doorway of the Garbhagṛha

The *lalātabimba* of the lintel depicted a four armed seated Nandīvāhana Śiva (Plate No.5) flanked by Brahmā on the right and Viṣṇu on the left side respectively. The lintel also depicted with attendant divinities in niches and recesses. The doorway has nine *śākhās,* the first and fourth *śākhā* has stencilled scrolls, second and sixth has dancing apsarās, the third and fifth with vyālas and the seventh is of mithunas, the eighth and ninth depicted with lotus petals, scrolls with nāga figures. The river goddesses Gaṅgā and Yamunā are depicted on the right and left jambs of the doorways. The niches below the *stambha śākhās,* depicted with the images of Śiva-Pārvatī while the niches below has nāga figures, musicians and dancers.

Garbhagṛha

The *garbhagṛha* of the temple is a square cella of 10 feet

wide and an oblong entrance and the ceiling supported on pilasters. All the pilasters have the usual type of shaft, capital and brackets supporting a beam and cornice. The monotony of the plain inner walls is relieved by a shelf on the north and a niche on the south side. A marble Śiva-Liṅga (Plate No.6) resting on a sandstone of *pīṭhika* is enshrined in the middle of the *garbhagṛha*. The *pīṭhikā* has the mouldings of *jāḍya kuṃbha, kalaśa* and *paṭṭikā* with recesses in between.

The exterior of the sanctum of the temple is of a *saptaratha* on plan and as well as in elevation, rests on a high basement with mouldings of *pīṭha* and *vedibandha*. The *pīṭha* mouldings consist of *jādya kuṃbha, karnikā, grāssa-paṭṭikā* and *antarapaṭṭa* depicted freizes of elephants, horses, men and miscellaneous scenes including erotic. The *vedibandha* is surmounted by the *jaṅghā,* the wall portion depicting two rows of sculptures of divinities and apsarās. The two rows are separated by a *madhya bandha* of *grāssapaṭṭikā*. The upper most *kapōta* supports the flat ceiling.

References

1. *Paramal Rāso,* II, verses 28 & 54, Ed.by.S.S.Dās, Kāśā Nāgarī Pracāriṇī Sabhā.
2. *A.S.R.*, Vol. 21, p.62, Krishna Deva, *Temples of Khajurāho,* New Delhi, 1991, pp. 370-371.

Chapter-IV

ART

General Observation on Sculptural Art and Iconography

The Chandella artists followed the classical Indian tradition which is open to the artistic influence from the east and the west, which is a combination of the sensuousness of Eastern Indian Art with the nervous angular modelling of the Western Indian idiom. Although it cannot be compared with the Classical Guptā Art in sublimity, depth of feeling and inner experience of the artist. The Khajurāho sculptures are completely liberated from their wall surface and stand out fully in round as vivid and enchanting lyrics of modelled beauty. The plasticy of the fully rounded and modelled form is replaced by sharp edges and pointed angles with a stress on horizontals, verticles and diagonals.

The artists of Khajurāho inspired by an ecstatic joy of living and a consuming passion for the physical beauty and reveals to admire the human body from the most fascinating angles which gives us fine profiles and the unusual three quarter profiles. The art of Khajurāho matches and surpasses the medieval school of Orissa, in some cases, revealing the sensuous and many sided charms of the human body.

The sculptures are divisible into five categories as follows :

(1) The first category comprises cult images executed almost completely in the round, which are generally enshrined

in the *garbhagṛha* of the temple. These cult images are generally in *samabhaṅga* posture and have a large *prabhāvali* at the back depicted with figures of attendant gods and goddesses. The cult images are fashioned out in strict confirmity with canonical formulae and prescriptions of proportion mentioned in the canons of iconography, with a few exceptions.

(2) The second category of sculptures comprises *Parivāra* (Familial); *Pārśva* (attendant); *Āvaraṇa Devatās* (enclosing divinities) and numerous categories of Gods and Goddesses. These are executed either in round or in high or medium relief, occurs in the niches or figures against the walls. The sculptures which are occuring in the niches are more formal and partake of the iconographic qualities of cult images of first category. The other figures of gods and goddesses, including those of Dikpālas are less formal and more free and are distinguishable from human figures only by their pecular headdress, *jaṭā,* or *kirīṭa* or *karaṇḍa mukuṭas,* mounts and attriburtes held in the hands.

(3) The third category comprises Apśarās (celestial dancers and Surāsundarīs (celestial beauties, which are finest, executed either in round or in high or medium relief, found on the *jaṅghā* and in the minor niches of the facades and on the pillars or ceiling brackets. The Apsarās are generally represented as dancing in various postures and as attendants of the higher divinities, represented with hands held in *añjalī mudrā* or as carrying lotus flower, mirror, garland, water jar, dress as offering to the deities. Whereas the Surāsundarīs are express common human moods, sentiments and fancies. These Surāsundarīs are invariably depicted as youthful beauties, wearing the choicest, gems and garments and full of winsome grace and charm. Some of the Apsarās shown as disrobing.

yawning, scratching the back, touching the breasts, rinsing water from the monkeys, writing a letter, playing a flute or vīṇā, applying collyrium etc.

(4) The Fourth category comprises of secular sculptures which includes domestic scenes, teachers and disciples, dancers and musicians and erotic couple or groups etc. Some of the erotic scenes are rare sensitiveness and warmth of human emotion, which transcend from the physical to the spiritual plane.

(5) The fifth category of sculptures consists of animals including Vyālas, which is a heraldic and fabulous beast, represented as a rampant horned lion with an armed human rider on the back, some are represented with heads of elephant, man, parrot, boar etc. These Vyāla figures in the recesses of *jaṅghā* and on the ***sukanśika*** are most typical and popular sculptural theme and is invested with a deep symbolism.

Iconography

The Chandella sculptures and artists strictly followed the cannonical formulae and iconographical prescriptions of proportions, postures and attributes while executing the icons and cult images. The cult images are executed almost completely in the round. The Chandella rulers were tolerant towards all the religion and creed. The utmost predominance was enjoyed by the Purāṇic religion with its idea of Trinity, that is, Brahmā, Viṣṇu and Śiva, as well as its innumerable myths and legends connected with different gods and goddesses.

The Kaṇḍariyā Mahādeva temple displays the sculptural representations of various forms of Śiva and Viṣṇu and also composite figures of Harīhara, Hariharapitāmaha, Harihara-Hiraṇyagarbha, Ardhanārīśvara etc. Some of the important icons and sculptures are described as follows :

SCULPTURES KEPT IN A NICHE ON THE OUTER AḌHIṢṬHĀNA

(a) Dancing Gaṇēśa kept in a niche on the south face or ardhamaṇḍapa (Plate No.7) — A sculpture depicting a ten armed dancing Gaṇēśa. All the hands except the lower left carrying scarf, broken. His head is broken and wears a torque, *hāra, śarpōpavīta, kēyūras,* wristlets, lower garment fastened by a belt with jewelled loops and tassel. The mount, rat is depicted between the feet of the god, nibbling at the hanging end of the central tassel of his garment. A flutist is depicted on the right side and a drummer on the left side of the god. The halo is depicted with a seated four armed goddess on the right side and a seated Saraśvati playing on Vīṇā, on the left side respectively.

(b) Dancing Cāmuṇḍā kept in a niche on the southern Face of the Maṇḍapa — A sculpture depicting a twelve armed dancing Cāmuṇḍā, as emaciated looking ugly and ferocious with protruding eyes, gaping mouth, prominent veins and bones, dried up hanging breasts and a sunken belly with a scropien. She is flanked by a *preta* on either side and stands on a human corpse. The *preta* on the proper left is munching up a human hand. She is also flanked by a seated goddess on either side of the halo.

(c) Dancing Indrāṇī kept in a niche on the southern transept of the Mahāmaṇḍapa — A sculpture depicting a four armed dancing Indrāṇī, holding *vajra, spiral, lotus, stalk* and other two hands are broken. Her mount, an elephant is depicted on the right side below. She wears a *jaṭāmukuṭa, kuṇḍalas,* torque with pendant, *hāra, kēyūras,* and *sārī* fastened by a belt with jewelled loops and tassels. She is flanked by a female attendant on either side carrying *kaṭ ihasta* and *cāmara.* On the left side, infront of female attendant depicted a seated devotee with hands held in *añjalī mudrā.* Behind the female *chaūri* bearer, shown a female attendant carrying garland in her hands. The halo is depicted with a seated goddess on either side.

(d) Dancing Varāhī kept in a niche on the southern transept of the garbhagṛha — A sculpture depicting a four armed dancing Varāhī, the counterpart of Varāha Viṣṇu. All the hands, portion below the bust and the muzzle of the goddess are broken and chipped off. Her mount, buffalo is depicted to the left side of the goddess as regardant. She wears a crown, torque, *kēyūras,* and *vanamālā,* on the surviving parts of her body. She is flanked by female attendant on either side, holding a *caurī* in one hand and other held in *kaṭihasta.* On either side of the halo is depicted with a four armed seated goddess.

(e) Dancing Vaiṣṇavī kept in a niche on the western transept of the garbhagṛha — A sculpture depicting a four armed dancing Vaiṣṇavī the counterpart of Viṣṇu. All the hands are broken except the lower right hand which is held in *abhayamudrā.* She wears a *kirīṭamukuṭa, kuṇḍalas,* torque with pendant, *hāra, kēyūras,* wristlets and *sārī* fastened by a belt with jewelled loops and tassels. She is attended by *Garuḍa* on the left side as regardant and a female attendant on the right. A kneeling devotee with folded hands in *añjali* *mudrā* depicted infront of Garuḍa. On either side of the halo is depicted with seated goddess.

(f) Dancing Kaumārī kept in a niche on the northern transept of the garbhagṛha — A sculpture depicting a dancing three headed and four armed Kaumārī, the consort of Kārttikeya. All the hands are broken except the upper left hand holds book. Her mount, peacock is shown with fully extended plumes in dancing attitude. She wears a crown on the principal head, torque, with pendant, *hāra, kēyūras,* wristlets, *sārī* fastened by a belt with a jewelled loops and tassels, long *mālā* coming below the knees. She is attended by a female attendant on either side and a male devotee seated with folded hands on the left side of the goddess. On either side of the halo is depicted with a four armed seated goddess, holding sword in one of the hands.

(g) Dancing Māheśvarī kept in a niche on the northern transept of Mahāmaṇḍapa — A sculpture depicting four armed dancing Māheśvarī, the counterpart of Māheśvara, carrying *abhayamudrā, triśūla, nāga,* and the fourth hand is broken. She wears a *jaṭāmukuṭa, kuṇḍalas,* torque with pendant, *hāra, kēyūras,* wristlets, *sārī,* long *mālā,* coming below the knees. She is attended by *Nandī* as regardant to the left side of feet and flanked by female attendant on either side. In the extreme lower right depicted a female attendant with *kaṭihaśta* and *kalaśa* while the left corner represented Ardhanārīśvara. The right half of Ardhanāriśvara represents female which is rather unusual. On either side of the halo is depicted with seated four armed goddesses.

(h) Dancing Brahmāṇī kept in a niche on the northern face of Maṇḍapa — A sculpture depicting a three headed and four armed dancing Brahmāṇī, the counterpart of Brahmā. She holds *śruk,* book and her other two hands are broken. Her mount goose is shown on the right of the feet of the goddess and a bearded ascetic with hands held in *añjali mudrā* on the left side. She wears crown and other usual ornaments on the body. She is attended by a female *caurī* bearer on either side.

(i) **Dancing Vīrabhadra kept in a niche on the northern face of Mukhamaṇḍapa** — A sculpture depicting a six armed dancing Vīrabhadra. All the hands are broken except the lower right hand holds scarf like object. He wears a *jaṭāmukuṭa, kuṇḍalas,* and other usual ornaments and dress on the body. A defaced Nandī is as regardant. He is attended by a seated drummer with two *mṛdaṅgas* placed diagonally across either other on the right and a standing flutiests on the left side. On either side of the halo is depicted with three headed and four armed Brahmā on the right and a seated four armed Viṣṇu on the left side.

SCULPTURES KEPT IN A NICHE IN THE INTERIOR MAHĀMAṆḌAPA STARTING FROM NORTH-EAST.

(a) **Catuṣpāda Mahā Sadāśiva** — A sculpture depicting a six headed, four legged and twelve armed Mahā Sadāśiva (Plate No.8) with some characteristics of Hariharapitāmaha, as is clear from the representations of the heads of *haṁsa, Nandī* and *garuḍa,* the mounts of Brahmā, Śiva and Viṣṇu respectively. Here, the Śiva form has been given more prominence as is evident from a Liṅga surmounting all the heads and the delineation of the third eye on the principal head. The deity is seated in *padmāsana,* is *ūrdhvāmedhrā,* makes it as a form of Śiva. The upper three heads adorned to the Liṅga, wears *jaṭāmukuṭa* while other two heads wears *kirīṭamukuṭa, kuṇḍalas,* torque, *kauṣtubhamaṇi, upavīta, kēyūras,* deer skin, lower garment fastened by a belt with jewelled loops and tassels, anklets, etc. The upper pair of legs are in *padmāsana* and the lower pair of legs is in *bhadrāsana.* All the hands are broken except the lower right hand holds *akṣamālā-cum-varada mudrā.*

A three headed and four armed pot bellied male deity is shown seated in *padmāsana* between the lower feet. The halo is flanked by a seated four armed Brahmā on the right and Viṣṇu on the left side respectively. The main deity, is flanked by a standing male attendant on either side, the right one holding *kaṭihasta* and *tṛśūla* while the left one holds *khaṭvāṅga* and *kaṭīhasta.*

(b) Brahmā and Brahmāṇī — A scultpure depicting Brahmā-Brahmāṇī seated in *lalitāsana* on a pedestal (Plate No.9). Brahmā is three headed and four armed, holding *śrūk, book* and embracing his consort with the lower left hand and the fourth one is broken. He has no beard and wears a peculiar headdress and wears *kuṇḍalas,* torque, *hāra, yajñopavīta,* lower garment etc. Brahmāṇī seated on the left lap, has typical headdress of dharmilla type and to ears torque with pendant, *hāra, kēyūras, sārī* with drapery ends on the left side. Her left foot placed on the lotus leaf, which is being adorned by a kneeling devotee with folded hands in *añjali mudrā.* They are attended by a female attendant on either side holding lotus flower and *kaṭihasta.* The halo is flanked by a seated deity on either side.

(c) Śiva and Pārvatī — Maheśvara, seated in *lalitāsana*

on a pedestal. Śiva has four arms, the right hands are broken while the upper left hand holds nāga and the lower left hand embracing Pārvatī. His head is also broken and wears *kuṇḍala*s, torque, *hāra, kēyūras,* wristlets, *upavīta,* long *mālā* and anklets. Umā seated on the left lap of Śiva and her right hand thrown on the shoulders of Śiva and embracing while her left hand is broken. She wears *kuṇḍalas,* torque with pendant, *kēyūras, hāra, sārī* and other ornaments etc. Her mount Lion is represented on the left side and Śiva's mount Nandī is represented on the right side. The deities are flanked by two male attendants on either side holding sword and *kaṭihasta.* The halo is depicted with a seated four armed Brahmā on the left side and the right side of the halo is broken.

(d) Kalyaṇasundara Mūrti of Śiva — A sculpture is depicting Śiva and Pārvatī as Kalyaṇasundara mūrti (Plate No.10). Pārvatī is shown standing on the right of Śiva. Her left hand holds a mirror while her right hand stretched towards the right hand of Śiva which is partly broken. She wears a *kirīṭamukuṭa, kuṇḍalas,* torque with pendant, *hāra,* wristlets, *sārī* fastened by a belt with jewelled loops and tassels and anklets.

Śiva is shown standing to right. All the four hands are broken except the upper right hand thrown on the Pārvatī's shoulder in emrace and holds a *nāga*. He wears a *jaṭāmukuṭa*, *kuṇḍalas,* torque, *hāra, kēyūras,* wristlets, *yajñopavīta,* lower garment, scarf, long *mālā,* anklets etc. Both are richly ornamented.

A four armed seated Brahmā is shown between the two figures at the back performing the marriage ceremony of Śiva and Pārvatī. A female attendant holding *curi* and *kaṭihasta,* shown on the right flanking of Pārvatī and a *Gaṇā* holding *khaṭvāṅga* and *kaṭihasta* stands on the left flank of Śiva. The mounts, Lion and Nandī are also depicted on the left and right side of the deities. In the extreme right corner is shown a male attendant and in the left a female attendant carrying garlands. On the top right is depicted Indra riding on an elephant and on the top left had Yama riding on buffalo. Four *mangala ghaṭas,* the water jars placed one above the other are shown on either side of the main deities, indicating the marriage scene of Śiva and Pārvatī.

SOUTH SIDE

(e) Śiva and Pārvatī — A sculpture depicting Śiva and Pārvatī and Umā-Maheśvara seated in *lalitāsana* on a pedestal. Śiva's head and all the hands are broken except the lower left hand which is embracing Pārvatī, who is seated on the left lap of Śiva. Pārvatī's right hand is embracing Śiva and her left hand is broken. Both are richly ornamented with usual dress on the bodies. Lion, the mount of Pārvatī is depicted on the front of the pedestal. A four armed seated Viṣṇu on the left side the halo and the right halo portion is broken.

(f) Brahmā and Brahmāṇī — A sculpture depicting Brahmā and Brahmāṇī seated in *lalitāsana* on a pedestal. Brahmā is three headed and four armed. All the hands are broken except the lower left hand embracing Brahmāṇī. He wears *jaṭāmukuṭa, kuṇḍalas,* torque, *hāra, yajñopavīta, upavīta, kēyūras,* lower garment and anklets. Brahmāṇī is embracing her Lord Brahmā with her right hand and left hand holds lotus stalk. She has typical dhammilla type of headdress and wears *kuṇḍalas*, torque with pendant, *hāra, yajñopavīta*, etc. Brahmāṇī is two armed and holding mirror in the left hand

and with her right hand she embracing her Lord Brahmā. She wears usual dress and ornaments on her body. The halo is flanked by a seated bearded ascetic with folded hands on either side.

(g) Garuḍavāhana Viṣṇu — A sculpture depicting a four armed Viṣṇu seated on his *vāhana,* Garuḍa in an anthropomorphic form with wings. All the hands and head of Viṣṇu are broken and wears torque, *hāra, kauśtubhamaṇi, yajñopavīta, kuṇḍalas,* lower garment and *vanamālā*. He is attended by a female attendant with folded hands in *añjali mudrā* on either side. The halo is depicted with three headed and four armed Brahmā on the right and seated four armed Śiva on the left side respectively.

(i) Narasiṃha — A sculture depicting a four armed Narasiṃha (Plate No.20) standing in *pratyalīḍāsana* posture with his left foot placed on a lotus stalk. He is represented as ripping open the belly of Hiraṇyākaśipu with his two lowest hands of which only the left one is intact. All the hands are broken except the uppermost right one tearing his hair. A male attendant wielding a staff is shown on either side of the gods feet. The halo is depicted with the seated four armed goddess on either side.

WEST SIDE

(j) Harihara — A sculpture depicting a four armed Harihara (Plate No. 11) standing in samabhaṅga posture on a pedestal. All the hands are broken and wears *jaṭāmukuṭa* on the right-half and *kirīṭamukuṭa* on the left-half, *kuṇḍalas,* torque, *kaustubhamaṇi, hāra, yajñopavīta, kēyūras,* lower garment, scarf, long *mālā* and anklets. He is flanked by standing *gaṇa* holding *khaṭvāṅga* and *kaṭihasta* on the right side and Lakṣ mī, the consort of Viṣṇu, holding stalk and *kaṭihasta,* on the left side. The mounts of the two gods, Nandī and Garuḍa are shown on the right and left respectively. The halo is depicted with four armed headless Brahmā on the right and Viṣṇu on the left side respectively.

(k) Ardhanārīśvara — A sculpture depicting a four armed standing Ardhanārīśvara (Plate No. 12). The head and all the hands are broken except the lower right hand held in *varadamudrā.* There is a trace of holding a *nāga* in the upper right hand. The deity wears a torque with pendant, *hāra, yajñopavīta, kēyūras,* wristlets, lower garment, scarf, long *mālā* and anklets. A breast is shown prominently on the left chest and the deity is flanked by four male attendants two each on either side and also a seated devotee with folded hands in *añjali mudrā* on either side. The halo is depicted with two armed deity carrying *abhayamudrā* and water vessel on either side.

(l) Śiva — A sculpture depicting a eight armed Śiva, standing in tribhaṅga posture on a pedestal. The head and all hands are broken and wears *kuṇḍalas,* torque, *hāra, yajñopavīta, kēyūras,* undergarment, scarf, long *mālā* and anklets. He is attended by a *gaṇas* on either side, the right one holds *khaṭvāṅga* and the left one holding *triśūla.* Behind the *gaṇas,* shown a female *caurī* bearer, on either side. The mount, Nandī is shown on the right side and a seated male devotee on the left side of the feet of the god. The halo is depicted with seated four armed Brahmā and four armed seated Viṣṇu on the right and left side respectively.

NORTH SIDE

(m) Brahmā and Brahmāṇī — A sculpture depicting a three

headed and four armed Brahmā, standing in *tribhaṅga* posture on a pedestal with his consort Brahmāṇī. All the hands of Brahmā are broken except the lower left hand embracing Brahmāṇī. He is bearded, potbellied and wears a *jaṭāmukuṭ a, kuṇḍalas,* torque, *hāra, yajñopavīta, kēyūras,* wristlets, lower garment, scarf, long *mālā* and anklets.

Brahmāṇī is shown to the left. Her hands are also broken and she wears *kuṇḍalas,* torque, *hāra, kēyūras,* wristlets, *sārī* fastened by a belt with jewelled loops and tassels and with drapery ends on the left side. Both are attended by a female *caurī* bearers and seated devotee on either side. The halo is depicted with four armed seated deities on either side probably Agni and Viṣṇu.

(n) Śiva and Pārvatī as Umā-Mahēśvara — A sculpture depicting Śiva-Pārvatī as Umā-Mahēśvara, seated in *lalitāsana* on their mounts Nandī and Lion. Śiva has four arms, holds *nāga,* in the upper left hand and the lower left hand is embracing Pārvatī while the other two hands are broken. He wears a *Jaṭāmukuṭa, kuṇḍalas* and other usual ornaments on the body.

Pārvatī has two arms, the left hand holds flower and the right hand is embracing her Lord Śiva. She wears as usual dress and ornaments on her body. Both are attended by a Śaiva *gaṇas* on either side, the left one holding *kapāla* and *khaṭvāṅga* while the right one holding *triśūla.* The halo is depicted with seated four armed Gaṇēśa on the right and another four armed deity on the left side.

(o) Bhairava — A sculpture depicting a Bhairava (Plate No.13) seated in *lalitāsana* on a pedestal. He is bearded, pot bellied and has protruding eyes and side tusks. All the hands are broken and wears a *Jaṭāmukuṭa,* studded with a series of skulls with arms, *kuṇḍalas,* torque, *hāra,* etc. He is attended by Nandī and a *gaṇa* on either side, the right one holding *khaṭvāṅga* and the left one holding triśūla. A seated devotee with folded hands in *añjali mudrā* are shown on either side. The halo is depicted with seated Brahmā on the right and a seated Viṣṇu on the left side respectively.

(p) Pārvatī — A sculpture depicting a four armed Pārvatī seated in *lalitāsana* on her mount, Lion. Her head and all the hands are broken and wears *kuṇḍalas,* torque, *sāri* fastened by a belt and anklets. She is attended by male attendant on either side on the top and at the below.

(q) Śiva and Pārvatī as Umā-Maheśvara — A scuipture depicting Śiva and Pārvatī as Umā-Maheśvara, seated in *lalitāsana* on a pedestal. Śiva has four arms, his right hands are broken while the upper left hand holds *nāga* and the lower left hand embracing his consort Pārvatī. He wears *Jaṭāmukuṭ a* and other usual ornaments and dress on the body Pārvatī and other usual ornaments and dress on the body. Pārvatī is seated and embracing her Lord Śiva with her right hand and the left hand holds a mirror. She wears as usual dress and ornaments on her body.

Gaṇēśa depicted on the right and Lion, the mount of Pārvatī, on the left side. Nandī and dancing *gaṇa* are depicted below the seat. A male attendant on the lower left holds *triśūla* and the right one holds *khaṭvāṅga.* The halo is depicted with seated Brahmā on the right and Viṣṇu on the left side respectively.

(r) Indra and Indrāṇi — A sculpture depicting Indra and

Indrāṇi seated in *lalītāsana* on a pedestal (Plate No.14). Indra has four arms, holds lotus stalk and embracing his consort Indrāṇi while other two hands are broken. He wears a short *karaṇḍamukuṭa,* torque with pendant, *hāra, yajñpavīta, kēyūras,* wristlets, undergarment and long *mālā.*

Indrāṇi has two arms, the right hand embracing her Lord Indra and the left hand is broken. She has typical dhammilla type of headdress and wears *kuṇḍalas,* torque with pendant, *hāra, kēyūras, sārī* and anklets. A female attendant holding garland is shown on either side at the extreme corner. The mount of Indra, an elephant is depicted below the seat and the halo is depicted with deity on either side.

(s) Bhairava — A sculpture depicting a eight armed Bhairava standing in tribhaṅga posture on a pedestal. He has raised curling hairs studded with a skull, protruding eyes, teeth, and whiskers. All the hands are broken, pot bellied and wears *kuṇḍalas,* torque, *hāra, yajñopavīta, kēyūras,* wristlets, lower garment, scarf and anklets. He is attended by male attendant on either side and below which depicts a seated devotee. A *gaṇa* and Nandi depicted on either side of the deity. The halo is depicted with seated four armed Brahmā on the left side and a seated four armed Viṣṇu on the right side respectively.

SCULPTURES KEPT IN A NICHE OF THE GARBHAGṚHA FACADES FACING INNER AMBULATORY

Southern Face

(a) Vaikuṇṭhanātha Viṣṇu — A sculpture depicting a three-headed and eight-armed Viṣṇu as Vaikuṇṭhanātha. He is standing in *tribhaṅga* posture on a pedestal. He holds lotus with stalk in the lower right hand, *cakra* in the upper right hand, *śaṅkha* in the lower left hand and the remaining five hands are broken and missing. The principal head is of human, Lion's head (Narasimha) on the right and Boar's head (Varāha) on the left. The deity wears a *kirīṭamukuṭa, kaustubhamaṇi, kuṇḍalas,* torque, *hāra, yajñopavīta, kēyūras,* wristlets, undergarment, scarf, and *vanamālā.* The *cakra* is addorsed an arrow with three miniature human heads. The deity is flanked by Garuḍa on the right side and Lakṣmi on the left and also attended by a male attendant and kneeling devotees on either side. The halo is depicted with Brahmā on the right and Śiva on the left side respectively.

(b) Indra — A sculpture depicting a four armed Indra, standing in posture on a pedestal. He holds *vajra, aṅkuśa, kamaṇḍala* and *kaṭihasta.* He wears *karaṇḍamukuṭa kuṇḍalas,* torque, *hāra, yajñopavīta, kēyūras,* wristlets, undergarment, scard and long *mālā* coming below the knees. The mount, elephant is depicted on the left side of the deity.

(c) Agni — A sculpture depicting a four armed Agni, standing in *samabhaṅga* posture on a pedestal. He is bearded and hands holds *śruk, book, varadamudrā,* and the fourth one is broken and missing. He wears *jaṭāmukuṭa, kuṇḍalas,* torque, *hāra, yajñopavīta, kēyūras,* wristlets, undergarment, scard and long *mālā* coming below the knees. A headless ram, the mount, of Agni is depicted on the left side of the deity.

(d) Andhakāsuravadha Mūrti of Śiva — A sculpture depicting a sixteen armed Andhakāsuravadha *mūrti* of Śiva (Plate No. 15), standing in *pratyālīḍāsana* posture. All the hands are broken except the upper right hand and left hands holds the skin of the elephant Gajasura, as a canopy over the head and the other left hand holds shield. He is shows in a ferocious attitude with bulging eyes, gaping mouth with protruding teeth and full whiskers. He wears a jaṭāmukuṭa, *kuṇḍalas,* torque, *hāra, yajñopavīta, kēyūras,* wristlets, undergarment, scard and *ruṇḍamālā.* His left foot crushed the monster and his consort also represented. The deity is attended by Nandi on the left side and an agitated four armed Cāmuṇḍa on the right side holding *triśūla,* dagger, *khaṭvāṅga* and *kapāla* wherein she is collecting the blood of demon. A seated headless devotee is shown the right side while a fallen demon depicted below the feet of Cāmuṇḍā. The halo is depicted with seated goddesses probably Śivānī on the right side and another seated goddesses on the left side respectively.

(e) Yama — A sculpture depicting a four armed Yama, holds a *kapāla* in one of the right hand and other hands are broken. His hairs are raised in curls studded with skulls, protruding eyes, gaping mouth and whiskers. He wears usual ornaments and dress on the body. He is attended by standing devotee with folded hands in *añjali mudrā* on either side and his mount, buffalo is depicted as regardant on the left side.

(f) Kubera and Kuberi — A sculpture depicting Kubera with his consort Kuberi, seate in *lalitāsana* on a pedestal. He has four arms and holds a wine cup, lotus stalk and money bag in his three hands and the fourth one is embracing his consort Kuberi. He wears *karaṇḍamukuṭa, kuṇḍalas,* torque, *hāra, yajñopavīta, kēyūras,* wristlets, undergarment fastened to a belt with loops and tassels, long *mālā* coming below the knees.

Kuberi is seated towards the left of Kubera. She has two

arms, the right hand embracing her Lord Kubera and the left hand holds lotus. She wears usual dress and ornaments on her body. The two jars representing *nidhis* on the left side of the deity and a male devotee seated with hands held in *añjali mudrā*. Just below the pedestal and on the right side corner depicting a female attendant holding garland in the hands. A seated four armed pot bellied deity is depicted on either side of the halo.

(g) Garuḍavāhana Viṣṇu — A sculpture depicting a four armed Viṣṇu (Plate No.16) seated in *lalitāsana* on an anthropomarphic form of Garuḍa, the *vāhana* of Viṣṇu. His hands carry *varada mudrā, gadā, cakra* and *śaṅkha* respectively. He wears a *kirīṭamukuṭa, kuṇḍalas,* torque, *hāra, yajñopavīta, kēyūras,* lower garment fastened by a belt with jewelled loops and tassels, long *mālā*. He is attended by *Śaṅkhapuruṣa* on the right and *Cakrapuruṣa* on the left side and also a seated devotee with folded hands in *añjali mudrā* on either side. The halo is depicted with seated four armed deity on either side.

(h) Vasu — A sculpture depicting a standing four armed bull faced Vasu. He holds *book, spiral lotus stalk, kamaṇḍal* and the lower right hand held in *varada mudrā*. He wears a short *karaṇḍamukuṭa, kuṇḍalas,* torque, *hāra, yajñopavīta, kēyūras,* wristlets, undergarment, scarf, long *mālā* coming below the knees. Nandi is depicted as regardant on the left side and on the right side a devotee seated folded hands in *añjali mudrā*.

Western Face

(i) Nirriti — A sculpture depicting a four armed Nirriti

standing in *tribhaṅga* posture on a pedestal. He is shown nude and holds sword and sickle in the two hands and other hands are broken. He wears a *jaṭāmukuṭa, sarpakuṇḍalas, sarpahāra, yajñopavīta,* and a long *mālā*. The mount, *Naravāhana* is shown reclining at reclining at the feet of the god.

(j) Naṭarāja Śiva — A sculpture depicting a sixteen armed Naṭarāja Śiva (Plate No.17), standing in dancing posture on a pedestal. The head, hands and portion below the bust of the deity are broken. The mount, Nandi is depicted on the left side of the pedestal. A dancing *gaṇa* depicted on either side and the halo is depicted with seated goddesses on the left one playing on Vīṇā and the right one playing on another instrument, on either side.

Northern Face

(k) Tripurāntaka Mūrti of Śiva — A sculpture depicting a sixteen armed Śiva as Tripurāntaka-mūrti of Śiva (Plate No.18), standing in *pratyālīḍāsana* posture. All the hands are broken except the upper two right hand holds triśūla and sword and the upper most left hand holds shield. A block of stone depicting three niches with a miniature figures in each on the front side, above the shield indictes symbolically represents tripuras, the three cities of the demons, namely, Vidyunmali, Tarakaśa and Kamalākṣa. The deity has third eye and wears a *jaṭāmukuṭa* and other usual ornaments and dress on the body. He is flanked by a four armed standing Gaṇēśa on the right side and a two armed Kārttikeya seated on the peacock, on the left side. The mount, Nandi is depicted as regardant on the left side of the deity.

(l) Gajalakṣmī — A sculpture depicting a four armed

Gajalakṣmī (Plate No.19) standing in *samabhaṅga* posture on a pedestal. The upper hands holds lotus stalk supporting elephant while the lower left hand held in *varadā mudrā* and the other one is broken. She wears a *karaṇḍamukuṭa, kuṇḍalas* and other ornaments on her body. She is attended by a standing female attendant on either side and a seated male devotee on either side.

(m) **Lakṣmī-Nārāyaṇa** — A sculpture depicting Lakṣmī-Nārāyaṇa (Plate No.20) seated in *lalitāsana* on a pedestal. Nārāyaṇa has four arms, holds *gadā, śaṅkha,* and the lower left hand embraces his consort Lakṣmī and fourth hand is broken. He wears a *kirīṭmukuṭa,* with other usual ornaments and dress on the body. Lakṣmī seated on the left lap of Nārāyaṇa, embraces her Lord with her right hand and the left hand holds a mirror. She has a *cakra* shaped headdress and wears usual ornaments and dress on her body. They are attended by a male attendant, seated devotee and a female attendant on either side. The halo is depicted with Brahmā and Śiva on the right and left side respectively.

(n) **Śiva and Pārvatī as Umā-Māheśvara** — A sculpture depicting Śiva and Pārvatī as Uma-Maheśvara (Plate No.21), standing in tribhaṅga posture on a pedestal. Śiva has four arms and carries *varada mudrā, triśūla, nāga,* in the three hands and the lower left hand embraces his consort Pārvatī. He wears a *jaṭāmukuṭa* with usual dress and ornaments on the body. Pārvatī standing to the left side of Śiva with her right hand embraces her Lord and left hand holds a mirror. She has a cakra shaped headdress and wears usual dress and ornaments on her body. The Nandi and Lion, mounts are depicted on the right and left side. The deity is flanked by Śaiva *gaṇas* on either side, the right one holding *khaṭvāṅga* and the left one holding *triśūla*.

SOME OF THE IMPORTANT SCULPTURES DISPLAYED AROUND THE JAṆGHĀ WALL PORTION STARTING FROM SOUTH-EAST

(a) Śiva — A sculpture depicting a four armed Śiva standing in *tribhaṅga* posture on a pedestal. He has four arms, carrying *varada mudrā, lotus stalk, Roma* and *kamaṇḍala*. He wears a *jaṭāmukuṭa, kuṇḍalas,* torque, *hāra, yajñopavīta,* wristlets, lower garment fastened by a belt with jewelled loops and tassels, a scarf and *mālā*. Nandi is shown on the left side as regardant.

(b) Indra — A sculpture depicting a four armed Indra, standing in *tribhaṅga* posture on a pedestal. His hands carrying *varadā mudrā, aṅkuśa, kamaṇḍala* and fourth one is broken. He wears a *karaṇḍamukuṭa, kuṇḍalas, hāra, yajñopavīta,* and other ornaments on the body. The mount, elephant is depicted on the right side of the feet as regardant.

(c) Agni — A sculpture depicting a four armed Agni. HIs hands carrying *varada mudrā, śruk, Roma* with *Roma* and *kamaṇḍala*. He is bearded, pot bellied and wears a *jaṭāmukuṭa, kuṇḍalas, hāra, yajñopavīta, kēyūras,* wristlets and other ornaments. His mount, Ram is depicted on the left side as a regardant and a devotee standing on the right side of the deity with hands held in *añjali mudrā*.

(d) Yama — A sculpture depicting a four armed Yama facing south. His hands carrying a *kapāla, damaru, khaṭvāṅga,* and a *bell*. He is depicted in a ferocious attitue with raised curls, studded with skulls, protruding eyes and moustaches. He wears *sarpakuṇḍalas,* torque, *hāra, yajñopavīta, kēyūras,* and long *mālā.* His mount Buffal is depicted as regardant on the left side and a male attendant on the right side of the deity.

(e) **Nirriti** — A sculpture depicting a four armed Nirriti, his hands carrying *Roma* and other two hands are broken. He is shown as *ūrdhvamedhra* and wears *jaṭāmukuṭa, kuṇḍalas, hāra, yajñopavīta* and long *mālā.* His mount, *Naravāhana,* a reclining human figure is depicted as regardant on the left side.

(f) **Varuṇa** — A sculpture depicting a four armed Varuṇa, standing in *tribhaṅga* posture on a pedestal. His hands carrying *varada mudrā, book,* partly encircled by a spiral lotus stalk, *kamaṇḍala,* and the fourth one is broken. His head is broken and wears *kuṇḍalas,* torque, *hāra, yajñopavīta, kēyūras,* lower garment, and long *mālā* coming below the knees. His mount, crocodile depicted as regardant on the right and a seated devotee with hands held in *añjali mudrā* on the left side of the deity.

(g) **Vāyu** — A sculpture depicting a four armed Vāyu, standing in *tribhaṅga* posture on a pedestal. His hands carrying *varada mudrā,Roma* and the fourth one is broken. He wears a *karaṇḍamukuṭa, kuṇḍalas, hāra, yajñopavīta,* under garment and long *mālā* coming below the knees. He is attended by a seated devotee with folded hands in *añjali mudrā* on either side and a deer couple on the left side of the deity.

(h) **Kārttikeya** — A sculpture depicting a four armed Kārttikeya standing in *dvibhaṅga* posture on a pedestal. His hands carrying *kaṭihasta, Roma* and fourth one is broken. He wears *karaṇḍamukuṭa, kuṇḍalas,* wristlets, undergarment, long *mālā,* coming below the knees. His mount, peacock is depicted on the left and a standing male devotee on the right side.

SCULPTURES KEPT IN THE NICHES OF THE ROOF PEDIMENTS

(a) Śiva and Pārvatī as Umā-Maheśvara — A sculpture depicting Śiva and Pārvatī as Umā-Maheśvara, kept in a niche on the roof pediment above the entrance *toraṇa* on the east. Both seated in *lalitāsana* on a pedestal. Śiva has four arms and carries *lotus flower, triśūla, nāga* and the lower left hand embraces Pārvatī. He wears a *jaṭāmukuṭa* and other usual ornaments and dress on the body. Pārvatī seated on the left lap of Śiva with her right hand embraces her Lord and the left hand holds a mirror. She has a typical dhammilla type of headdress and other usual dress and ornaments on her body. The mounts Nandi and Lion are depicted below the pedestal with a dancing *gaṇa* in between. The halo is depicted with seated deith on either side.

(b) Śiva and Pārvatī as Umā-Maheśvara — A sculpture depicting Śiva Pārvatī as Umā-Maheśvara, kept in a niche of the roof pediment over the *mukhamaṇḍapa,* seated in a *lalitāsana* on the pedestal. Śiva has four arms and carries *varadā mudrā, triśūla, nāga* and the lower left hand embraces Pārvatī. He wears a *jaṭāmukuṭa* with usual dress and ornaments. Pārvatī seated on the left lap with her right hand embraces her Lord and left hand holds a mirror. She too wears usual dress and ornaments on her body. Nandi depicted below the seat of the pedestal.

(c) Kārttikeya — A sculpture depicting a four armed Kārttikeya, kept in a niche of the pediment over *maṇḍapa*. He has three head, seated in *lalitāsana* on his mout peacock. His hands carries *fruit, lotus stalk, Roma* and *Śakti*. He wears *kirīṭamukuṭa, kuṇḍalas,* torque, *hāra, yajñopavīta,* and lower garments.

(d) Bhairava — A sculpture depicting Bhairava seated on Nandi, kept in a niche facing east. He is pot bellied and four armed, carrying *varadā mudrā, triśūla, khaṭvāṅga* and *kapāla*. He has raised flame like shaped curling hairs, protruding eyes and teetch.

(e) Kubera — A sculpture depicting kept in a niche of the southern face of the pediment of the *mahāmaṇḍapa*. He has four arms, carries a wine cup, lotus stalk, spira lotus stalk and a mongoose parose. He is pot bellied and wears crown, *kuṇḍalas,* and other ornaments.

(f) Pārvatī — A sculpture depicting kept in a niche of the western face of the pediment. She has four arms and standing in *samabhaṅga* posture. Her hands carrying varadā mudrā, lotus flower, lotus flower and *kamaṇḍala*. She wears as usual dress and ornaments. She is attended by female attendant and seated devotee on either side.

SCULPTURES KEPT IN NICHES OF THE ŚUKANĀSIKA

East Face

(a) Śiva — A sculpture depicting a standing four armed Śiva. His hands carries *varadā mudrā, triśūla, khaṭvāṅga* and the fourth one is broken. He wears *jaṭāmukuṭa* and other usual ornaments and dress on the body.

(b) Vaikuṇṭhanātha — A sculpture depicting a three headed and ten armed Viṣṇu as Vaikuṇṭhanātha, standing in *tribhaṅga* posture on a pedestal. His hands carry *varadā mudrā, cakra, shield* and the remaining hands are broken. He wears *kirīṭamukuṭa* and other usual ornaments and dress on the body.

(c) Śiva — A sculpture depicting a standing four armed Śiva. His hands carries *varada mudrā Roma akṣamālā, triśūla, nāga* and fourth one is broken. He wears a *jaṭāmukuṭa* and usual dress and ornaments on the body. He is attended by a couple of devotees on either side.

South Face

(d) Gaṇeśa and Vighneśvarī — A sculpture depicting Gaṇeśa with his consort Vighneśvarī, seated in *lalitāsana* on a pedestal. He has four arms, carries, *cakra, paraśu, nāga* and the lower left hand embraces his consort Vighneśvarī. He wears *karaṇḍamukuṭa* and other usual ornaments and dress on the body. Vighneśvarī seated on the left lap of Gaṇeśa. Her right hand embraces her Lord Gaṇeśa and left hand holds a mirror. She too wears usual ornaments and dress on her mount. The mount, Rat is depicted below the left foot of the god.

(e) Brahmā and Brahmāṇi — A sculpture depicting Brahmā and Brahmāṇi seated in *lalitāsana* on a pedestal. Brahmā is three headed and four hands, carries *kamaṇḍala, śruk, Roma* and lower left hand embraces his consort Brahmāṇi. He wears a *jaṭāmukuṭa* and other ornaments as usual. Brahmāṇī seated on the left lap of Brahmā with her right hand embraces her Lord and left hand holds a mirror. She wears *kuṇḍalas* and other usual ornaments and dress on her body. The mount, goose is depicted below the seat.

(f) Pārvatī — A sculpture depicting a four armed Pārvatī seated in *lalitāsana* on a pedestal. Her hands carries *varada mudrā, triśūla, lotus* and *kamaṇḍala*. She wears a *jaṭāmukuṭ a, kuṇḍalas* and other ornaments as usual. The halo is depicted with seated deity on either side.

West Face

(g) Śiva and Pārvatī as Umā-Maheśvar — A sculpture depicting Śiva and Pārvatī as Umā-Maheśvara, seated in *lalitāsana* on a pedestal. He has four arms and carried *lotus flower, triśūla, nāga* and the lower left hand embraces his consort Pārvatī. He wears a *jaṭāmukuṭa* and other ornaments and dress on the body. Pārvatī seated on the left lap of Śiva with right hand embraces her Lord and left hand holds a mirror. She has a typical dhanmilla type of headdress and wears usual ornaments and dress on her body. Both Nandi and Lion, the mounts of Śiva and Pārvatī are depicted below the seat.

(h) Viṣṇu — A sculpture depicting a four armed Viṣṇu standing in *samabhaṅga* posture on a pedestal. His hands carries a *varada mudrā, gadā, cakra* and *śaṅkha*. He wears a *kirīṭamukuṭa,* and other usual ornaments and dress on the body. He is flanked Cakrapuruṣa and Śaṅkhapuruṣa on the left and right side and also a seated devotee on either side of the deity.

North Face

(i) Viṣṇu — A sculpture depicting a four armed Viṣṇu

seated in *lalitāsana* on a pedestal. His hands carry *varada mudrā, gada, cakra* and *śaṅkha*. He wears a *kirīṭamukuṭa, kuṇḍalas, yajñopavīta* and other ornaments on the body. He is flanked by Śaṅkhapuruṣa and Cakrapuruṣa on either side and Garuḍa, the *vāhana* of Viṣṇu is depicted below the seat.

(j) Balarāma — A sculpture depicting a four armed Balarāma, seated in *lalitāsana* on a pedestal under a canopy of serpent hoods. His hands carries a *wine cup, mūśala, book* and *hala,* the plough share. He is shown well built body and wears a *karaṇḍamukuṭa* and other usual ornaments and dress on the body.

(k) Bhairava — A sculpture depicting a eight armed Bhairava seated in *lalitāsana* on a mount, Nandi. He is pot bellied, bearded and wears *jaṭāmukuṭa* and other ornaments. His hands carry *kapāla, triśūla, paraśu, ḍamaru* in the right hands while *khaṭvānga, ghanta, bow* and *kamaṇḍala* in the left hands respectively.

(l) Yogāsana Viṣṇu — A sculpture depicting a four armed Viṣṇu seated in *yogāsana* on a pedestal. He wears a *kirīṭ amukuṭa, kuṇḍalas,* and other usual ornaments on the body. His two lower hands held in *dhyāna mudrā* and the other two upper hands holds lotus flower with stalks.

North-East Corner

(m) Lakṣmī Nārāyaṇa — A sculpture depicting Lakṣmi Nārāyana seated in *lalitāsana* on a pedestal. Nārāyaṇa is four armed and holds *śaṅkha, gadā, cakra* in the three hands and the lower left hand embraces his consort Lakṣmī. He wears a *kirīṭamukuṭa* and other usual ornaments and dress on the body. Lakṣmī seated on the left lap of Nārāyaṇa with her right embraces her Lord and left hand holds lotus flower. She too wears usual ornaments and dress on her body.

(n) Śiva and Pārvatī as Umā-Maheśvara — A sculpture depicting Śiva and Pārvatī as Umā-Maheśvara, seated in *lalitāsana* on a pedestal. Śiva has four arms, holds *lotus flower, triśūla, nāga* in the three hands and the lower left hand embraces his consort Pārvatī who is seated on the left lap. He wears a *jaṭāmukuṭa* and other usual ornaments and dress on the body. Pārvatī has two arms, her right hand embraces her Lord Śiva and the left hand holds a mirror. She has a typical dhammilla type of headdress and wears usual ornaments and dress on her body. Both Nandi and Lion, the mounts are also depicted below the feet of the gods with a dancing *gaṇa* in between.

(o) Nandi Vāhana Śiva — A sculpture depicting a four armed Śiva seated on his mount, Nandi. His hands carries *varada mudrā, triśūla, lotus flower Roma stalk* and *kamaṇḍala*. He wears a *jaṭāmukuṭa* and other usual ornaments and dress on the body.

(p) Brahmā — A sculpture depicting a three headed and a four armed Brahmā, standing in *samabhaṅga* posture on a pedestal. His hands carries *varada mudrā, śruk, book* and *kamaṇḍala*. He is a pot bellied, bearded and wears a *jaṭāmukuṭ a* and other ornaments and dress on the body.

(q) Agni — A sculpture depicting a four armed Agni seated in *lalitāsana* on his mount, ram. He is a pot bellied bearded and wears a *jaṭāmukuṭa* and other usual ornaments and dress on the body. His hands carries *varada mudrā, śruk, book* and *kamaṇḍala*.

THE SOCIAL LIFE AND SOCIETY DEPICTED IN SCULPTURES

The social condition and life of the people during the Chandella period is depicted on this temple through sculptures and friezes which throw an interesting side light. The Khajurāho art is rich in representation of scenes portraying musicians and dancers in groups, hunting excensions, animal fights, royal processions, movements of armies and also domestic life. These artistic representations furnish some information about the nature of the costumes and ornaments, musical instruments, military weapons and also domestic impliments which were used by the people during the Chandella period. The artists selected their subjects from various aspects of life, individual and collective, representing them into the art prevalent during their time.

The artisans, sculptors, architects are depicted on the *adhiṣṭhāna*. Some of the senior architects represented as bearded and shows either standing or seated and surrounded by admiring crow of disciples. The hunting scenes are frequently quently depicted on the friezes and the hunters represented together with men, carrying on poles, hunted animals like boar and deer, wrestlers, acrobats and gladiators fighting elephants and lions are also depicted.

The dancing girls, belonged to the professional class of courtesans, who formed an important element of the contemporary society. These dancing girls depicted vaunting their charms and offering wine to their dupes. The prostitutes formed an allied class who are largely represented in naked erotic scenes on the friezes of the exterior and interior walls of the temple. The erotic sculptures portray in high relief intimate forms of amorous dalliance and sexual enjoyment.

These erotic scenes depicted may remind one of the art of love making technically treated in the Vātsayāna's Kāmasūtra. The barbers are used as attendants of female figures, for carrying a bag, slung from their shoulder, holding a mirror, toilet equipments, to extract thorns, paint the feet etc.

The Chandella army consisted of three principal arms, namely, infantry, cavalry and elephants. The cavalry do not seem to constitute a regular arm, although camels appear together with elephants, horses and foot men. The main weapon wielded by army are sword and shield, dagger and lances. The sword and round shield being very popular, exhibit many varieties. Although bow and arrow are also used by the army but these two weapons are generally used for hunting purpose. The numerous scenes of armies on march, the horses and elephants are depicted with or without riders, followed by footmen carrying arms are depicted on the *adhiṣṭhāna*.

The representation of military parades and rallies are of a cermonial nature. The secular processions are marked by gaiety and reverry, dance and music whereas the religious processions represent devotees going out on a pilgrimage depicted with gaily accoutered horses and elephants, flags and banners etc.

The amusements like huntings, wrestling, elephant fights, dance, music, drinking and acrobatics are among the popular amusements depicted on friezes of the temple walls and on the *adhiṣṭhāna*. Musical and dance performances were common recreations followed by drinking. Playing with ball was also another popular and favourite sport with the fair sex. The deer hunting and pig sticking was also another popular game during the times. The tigers were hunted with javeline from the elephant back. The friezes depicting elephant running amuck and trampling men under the feet or tearing or tossing up the unwary with the trunk, are frequently depicted on the *grāsspaṭṭikā* of the *adhiṣṭhāna*. The elephants chasing men and fight between elephants are also popular and was a favourite medieval sport conducted under the royal patronage.

Erotic Sculptures

The erotic sculptures on the temple lent themselves to various interpretations and evoked critism from some quarters. Some regard them as pornographical representations mirroring lax moral standards of the contemporary society. Others considered as illustrations of erotic postures mentioned in the *Kāmasūtra*. According to some says that Tāntric sects, the controlled enjoyment of senses was asurer as well as easier way to salvation but another view considers the physical union between man and woman as a symbolical expressions of Puruṣ a and Prākriti which is the sources of all life and creation.

According to Hindū philosophy, the moksha or liberation consists in the merging of the *ātman* with *paramātman,* the individual soul with the universal. The union of man and woman wherein all sense of duality is lost is represented on the temple to constitute a symbol of liberation. As the temples were dedicated to the search of the Supreme, these artistic creations and exuberant manifestations of the creative urge should have sprung from deep rooted traditions with a possible religious sanction. It is also suggested that these represents the erotic practices which invested sex with a ritual symbolism and considered Yoga, the spiritual exercise and Bhoga, the physical pleasure, to be alternature paths leading to the same goal, the attainment of final deliverence.

The representation of erotic scenes on the temple, was

regarded as a normal and natural because *Kāma* or pursuit of pleasure was deemed to be one of the four *puruṣārtha* or the aims of life and was regarded as an essential and indispensable, preliminary and a stepping stone to *mokṣa*. The physical union between man and woman, is indeed a human counterpart of the cosmic function of creation. The joy of physical union thus symbolically reflects the infinite joy of divinity in creation.

The erotic scenes of both pre-coital and coital varieties are depicted on the *jaṅghā,* in the niches of roof and on the processional friezes of the basement on the exterior and on the pillars, architraves, ceilings, doorjambs on the *jaṅghā* and the basement friezes of the *garbhagṛha* proper in the interior. This temple displays erotic scenes on all the registers, presenting the most vivid erotic spectacles. These display a coital couple accompanied by two to four attendants who participate in the love play either actively or positively.

The erotic scene depicted on the south vestibule is of coital pair, namely, the female climbing up the la of the standing male partner, assisted by a nude maid on the proper right and by a male attendant in tumescence of the left. The coital couple is identical in all the three panels, the only difference is in the detailed rendering of stance of the attendants, while the flanking maids on the top and bottom panels are nude, that on the middle panel is shown as disrobing herself and exposing her nudity.

The north vestibule displays variant scenes in all the three registers (Plate No.22). The uppermost depicts a pre-coital couple with aristocratic male wearing long curls a goatee bearded and a tira tenderly foundling his partner. The couple is flanked by a maid exposing her nudity and is also helped by a male attendant in the tumescene, standing on the left. The middle panel depicts a standing coital couple, is helped by a nude maid standing on the right by a nude male attendant in tumescence standing on the left. On the bottom register depicts a coital couple with the nude partner, having a short beard in the head down pose, being actively assisted by two nude standing maids, while the female partners entwines her arms round the necks of the two maids, the male partner presses both his palms on the exposed genitals of the maids.

The universal acceptance of the erotic motif in the religious part of India has, however, a deeper significance touching the roots of the Indian culture. It is important to recall that the creation myths from the Vedic age onwards have stressed on the popularity between the sexes as the sources of creations. According to Hindu view the final aim of life is salvation which lies in the merging of the *ātman* with *paramātman,* that is, the individual soul with the universal. The union of man and woman, wherein all sense of duality is lost, thus come to constitute a symbol of liberation.

The temple being a monument of manifestation, is structural symbolism leads from a broad base to a point. Sex forming an important element of the broad base of life, is therefore aptly depicted on the temple and such depiction is not at all in conflict with the supreme object or the final aim of life.

Apsarās or Surāsundarīs

Among the sculptures, the Apsarās constitute one of the finest and most numerous, executed either in round or in high or medium relief, on the *jaṅghā* and in the minor niches of the facades and on the pillars or ceiling, brackets or the recesses between the pillars in the interior. These apsarās invariably represented as handsome and youthful nymphs, attired in the choiest gems and garments, full of winsome grace and charm. They are depicted as dancing in various postures and also with carrying the lotus flower, mirror, water jars, raiments, ornaments offering etc. as offering for the divinities as attendants. These apsarās are portrayed to express common human moods, emotions and activities. Some shown as disrobing, yawning, scratching the back, touching the breasts, rinsing water from the wet plaits hair, removing thorns, founding a baby, playing with pets like parrots and monkeys, writing a letter, playing a flute or vīṇā, painting, applying collyrium etc.

The Apsarā figures of this temple are slender and have larger and thinner legs, the bust is definitely less heavy when compared with the Apsarās of Lakṣmaṇa temple, Khajurāho. Most of the Apsarās are seen standing in *tribhaṅga* posture seem wearing a headdress resembling *karaṇḍamukuṭa*. Some of the Apsarā figures of this temple are masterpieces of mediaeval sculptural art. An Apsarā figure on the south-east facade, is shown removing thorn, she balances her supple body on the right leg and rhythimically turns round to remove a thorn from the upraised left foot as though in a dance pose. Her body below the waist is seen in full back view while her bust and head turned in three-fourth profile. An Apsarā figure on the south facade shown standing in three-quarter back view with her bust turned round in profile, supports her left breast with her left hand while she scratches the back with her flexed right hand.

There are two Apsarā figures in the *mahāmaṇḍapa,* one represents a dancer in a complex pose, in the north-eastern corner and another Apsara represents standing gracefully under a canopy of spiral lotus stalks, playing on a flute.

Chapter-V

CONCLUSION

The Kaṇḍariyā Mahādeva temple is onen of the largest, and loftiest and finest monument of Khajurāho of Chandella dynasty. Its mature plan and design, grand dimensions and symmetrical proportions, superb sculptural embellishment and architectural elaboration, marks the most evolved and finished achievements of the Central Indian building style and one of the sublime creations of Indian architecture.

This temple is dedicated to Śiva, enshrining a marble Śiva-Liṅga. This is one of the fully developed temple consists on plan of the *mukhamaṇḍapa, maṇḍapa, mahāmaṇḍapa* with lateral transept, *aṅtarāla* and *garbhagṛha* enclosed by an inner ambulatory with transepts on the sides and on the rear. This is the only temple which has preserved two *makaratoraṇas,* one at the main entrance and another at the entrance of *mahāmaṇḍapa,* with exquisite designs.

Of all the temples, this temple has the loftiest basement with the most numerous and elegantly ornamented moulding, which includes two rows of processional friezes teeming with elephants and horses, warriors and hunters, acrobats and musicians, dancers and devotees and miscellaneous scenes including erotic couples. The largest number of sculptures of alluring beauty appear of the three bands of its wall and represents an animated arrāy of gods and goddesses, mithunas and surāsundarīs. The sculptures on this temple are conspicuously slender and taller and show richest variety of Apsarās in lively and often violently agitated postures. Exhibiting a mastery in the rendering of female contours and revealing a peak of conscious sophistication and exuberant grace, represents the highest watermark of the characterstic art-diction of Khajurāho.

The Kaṇḍariyā Mahādeva temple assigned to later part of Vidyādharas reign or to circa 1025-50 A.D. support is lent to this suggestion by the find of a short epigraph on a *maṇḍapa* pilaster of this temple, mentioning a king called Virimda, which may have been a pet name of Vidyādhara.

BIBLIOGRAPHY

Alexander Cunningham	Archaeological Survey of India Report, Vols. II, VII & XXI (Reprinted by Gayatri Offset Press), Indological Book House, New-Delhi, 1972
Das, S.S.	Ed. by. Paramāla Rāso, Kasinagari Pracharini Sabhā.
Krishna Deva	Temples of Khajurāho, Vols.I & II, Archaeological Survey of India, New Delhi, 1990.
Khanna, Ashok	Rhythm in Khajurāho, New Delhi, 1997
Mahdi Hussain	Ed. by. The Rehla of Ibun Battuta, Gaekwad's Oriental Series, CXXII, Baroda, 1953.
Ray, H.C.	Dynastic History of Northern India, Calcutta, 1936.
Sachan	Tans. by. *Alberunis India*, London.
Suresh, K.M.	Saivite Sculpture of Khajurāho.
Suresh, K.M.	Iconography of Viṣṇu of Khajurāho.

GLOSSARY

Adhiṣṭhāna	Basement of a temple, supporting a wall, pillar on pilaster and consisting of distinct moulded tiers.
Agni	The god of fire and guardian of the south-east point of the compass.
Āmalaka	A fluted meon shaped member crowning the Northern śikhars. It is a cognizance of Northern śikhara and surmounted by candrikā, kalaśa and vijaypūraka.
Andaka	Sikhara as a unit. A śikhara unenumbered by aṅgaśikharas is called ekanda, a śikhara addorsed by four ura shriṅgas is called pañcandaka and so on.
Aṅgaśikhara	Smaller śikhara addorsed to the main sikhara.
Antarāla	Vestibule, intermediate passage between *garbhagṛha* and maṇḍapa.
Antarapatta	Recessed moulding of the basement ornamented with a decorative device or figures in relief.
Apsarās	Heavenly nymph.
Ardhacandra	Half moon, the ornamental semi-circular step before a shrine doorway.
Ardhamaṇḍapa	Portico, entrance porch or compartment

	infront of the shrine of the main hall of a temple.
Āsana paṭṭa	Seat side coming between the vedika and the sloping parapet, the kakṣāsana.
Avatāra	An incarnations of Viṣṇu.
Āyatana	Temple, shrine, mandira.
Bada	Orissan term meaning wal or cubical portion of a temple below the śikhara.
Bandana	Orissa term meaning the set of mouldings binding the registers of the jaṅghā.
Barāṇḍā	Orissan term meaning the crowning set of mouldings of the bada or cubical portion of a temple, mouldings separating the jaṅghā from the śikhara, the same as varandika.
Beki	Orissan term for griva, the constricted cylindrical member above the śikhara and below the āmalaka.
Bhadra	Central projection of the jangha of the sanctum or maṇḍapa.
Bhāga	Unit of a division or specification.
Bhairava	The terrific form of Śiva.
Bhūmi	Storey, usually applied to each horizontal stage of the śikhara demarcated by a bhūmi āmalaka.
Bhūmi āmalaka	Āmalaka indicating a bhum, usually found on the karṇa ratha of the śikhara.
Bhūta	Crowning atlas-like goblin represented as carrying the load of a structure.
Brahmā	The first deity of the Hindū Trinity.
Brahmāṇī	The Śakti or female counterpart of Brahmā.
Caitya	The term applied to the arched roof caves of Buddhist or same as kudu.

Cakra	Discus, the emblems of Viṣṇu.
Cāmuṇḍa	The Śakti, the female counterpart of Yama.
Candra śilā	Moon stone, semi-circular of half-moon shaped step before a shrine.
Candrikā	An architectural member resembling a flattened bell and surmounting the āmalaka. It is also called in Orissan khapuri.
Deva	A god.
Devi	A goddess.
Deva koṣṭa	Niche on a temple wall enshring an image.
Diggaja	One of the elephants said to guard and preside over the four or eight cardinal points.
Dikpālas	The eight guardians of the eight points of the compass.
Durgā	A name of Pārvatī.
Dvārapala	Door keeper.
Gaja-Lakshmī	The goddess of Lakṣmī as represented with two elephants, one on either side of her, pouring water upon her head from vessels in their trunks.
Gajathāra	Frieze of elephants on the basement of a temple.
Gaṇa	Śiva's attendant generally represented as pot bellied.
Gaṅgā	The river Gaṅgēś, personified as goddess.
Ganapati or Gaṇeśa	The god of wisdom and son of Śiva and Pārvatī.
Gaṇa śākhā	A śākhā of the doorway ornamented with gaṇa figures represented as dancing or playing on musical instrument or froliking.
Garbhagṛha	Innermost chamber of a temple where the main deity is enshrined, also called sanctum sanctorum or cella.

Ghatapallava	Design of vase and foliage, usually found on pillars and pilasters.
Gopura	South Indian term meaning a gateway, a storyed structure over the main entrance through the enclosing walls to the premises of a temple.
Grāsapaṭṭikā	An architectural frieze of ornamental lion faces known as grāsa or kīrttimukha.
Grīvā	Neck, the constricted cylendrical member below the āmalaka.
Gandi	Orissan term for śikhara.
Ghaṇṭā	Bell-shaped member in the finial of pyramidal śikhara or pīḍha type.
Indra	The Lord of gods and guardian of east.
Indrāṇi	The Śakti, the female counterpart of Indra.
Jadya kuṁbha	A distinctive padma-like moulding of the jagati or adhiṣṭhāna.
Jagamohana	Orissan term for the maṇḍapa, usually a pīḍha duel infront of the sanctum.
Jagati	High platform.
Jaṇghā	The central portion of the temple wall, plain or decorated with a broad band of sculptures.
Kalaśa	A pot, also pot-like finial of the spire of a temple.
Karṇa mañjarī	Miniature replica of the main śikhara occuring on the corner projections.
Karṇa śriṅga	Same as karṇa mañjari.
Karṇa ratha	The ratha of the corner, projection on the angle of the temple.
Karṇikā	A knife edge moulding usually formed on the basement and pillar.

Khura	Lowest moulding of the adhiṣṭhāna and mandovara, also called upana in South India.
Kīrttimukha	Originally represented as a lion's face usually shown within a caitya window, also known as simhamukha, kīrttimukha-vaktra.
Kubera	The god of wealth and guardian of south.
Kuberi	The Śakti, the female counterpart of Kubera.
Kudu	The Tamil term meaning nest or a caitya arch motif.
Kuṅbha	Tall vase-shaped moulding placed above the khura mouldings.
Kuṭā	South Indian term meaning a shrine of square plan with a domical four-sided roof and a single finial.
Lalāṭabimba	Crest figure, central figure (image) of the door lintel generally representing a significant replicat or associate of the main deity enshrined in the sanctum.
Lakṣmī	The consort of Viṣṇu and goddess of wealth.
Lakṣmī-Nārāyaṇa	Lakṣmī with Nārāyaṇa-Viṣṇu, generally she is represented as seated on the left lap of Viṣṇu or standing to the left side.
Liṅga	The genital organ of Śiva, worshipped in the form of phallus.
Madhya bandha	Paṭṭika like horizontal projection dividing an architectural member into zones.
Mahādeva	A favourite epithet of Śiva as 'Great God'.
Mahā-maṇḍapa	Large enclosed hall infront of the main shrine, a maṇḍapa with lateral transepts usually showing balconied openings on Central and Western Indian temples.
Mahiṣamardinī	Durgā, who killed the demon Mahiṣāsura.

Makaratoraṇa	An ornamental entrance decorated with a festoned or garland issuing from the mouths of makaras placed over the capitals of the supporting columns or pilasters.
Maṇḍapa	Hall with or without pillars infront of the garbhagṛha. The maṇḍapa is placed between the ardhamaṇḍapa and mahāmaṇḍapa in a developed temples of Khajurāho.
Mithuna	Couple.
Mithuna sakha	A sakha of the doorway ornamted with mithuna figures.
Mukha-maṇḍapa	Front portico, entrance porch.
Mukuṭa	Crown or kirīṭa over the head of a deity.
Mūla-mañjari	The steam of the main śikhara.
Nāga	Serpent, snake.
Nāga-sakha	A sakha of the doorway ornamented with naga, serpent.
Nandi	The sacred bull, the vāhana of Śiva.
Nara-sakha	The doorway ornamented with human figures.
Narasiṁha	The Man-Lion, one of the incarnations of Viṣṇu.
Naravāhana	The reclining human figure, the vehicle of Nirritti.
Nārāyaṇa	The other name and other form of Viṣṇu.
Naṣṭa-mañjari	Incomplete representation of a miniature replica of the main śikhara, occuring as its decoration.
Nāsika	A minor projection or reentrant angle of bhadra.
Naṭarājạ	Śiva in his roll as dancer.
Navaraṅga	Maṇḍapa with four central and twelve periperial pillars enclosing nine ankanas.

Nava-ratha	A temple with nine rathas, or main verticale projections.
Nava-sakha	A door with nine sakhas.
Nirandhara-prāsāda	A temple without inner ambulatory or without pradakṣināpatha of the garbhagṛha.
Nirriti	The guardian of the south-west corner and personification of decay or destruction.
Padma	Lotus flower.
Padma-bandha	Broad band of decoration between rows of lotus petals on a pillar.
Pañcāyatana	A five shrined temple or a temple with four subsidiary shrines at the corners with main temple at the centre. The developed temples of Khajurāho are pañcāyatana, examples, Temples of Lakṣmaṇa, Viśvanātha and Kaṇḍariyā Mahādeva.
Pañca-ratha	A temple of five rathas or five main verticale projections.
Pañca-sakha	A doorway with five sakhas.
Pārvatī	The Śakti, the female counterpart of Śiva.
Pattikṣa	A major rectilinear moulding.
patralata	Ornament representing a creeper of scrolls.
Pīḍha	Pyramidal roof, or constituent unit resembling eaves or tiers.
Pīṭha	Pedestal or base for Śiva-Liṅga.
Potika	Corbel bracket over pillar.
Pradakṣiṇā	Circumambulation.
Pradakṣinā patha	Processional passage or ambulatory. The inner ambulatory is also called andharika.
Prati-ratha	Major projection of a nava-ratha śikhara.
Prati-karṇa	Projection flanking the karṇa-ratha.
Rājasena	Moulding supporting the vedikā of a kakṣāsana.

Ratha	The central verticle projection of the śikhara called Ratha or Ratha paga in Orissa.
Rekhā	Profile of a curvilinear spire or śikhara.
Rūpa-sakha	A sakha of the doorway decorated with figure carvings.
Sakha	Ornamental frame or jamb of a door.
Śalabhañjikā	Motif representing a beautiful young woman standing in tribhaṅga posture and holding the bunch of a tree which quickens to her touch.
Salilantara	Recessed change between projections on the temple facade.
Sandhara	A temple with an andharika or covered inner ambulatory arround garbhagṛha.
Sapta-ratha	A temple with seven ratha or main vertical projection.
Sapta-sakha	A door with seven sakhas.
Śārdūla	A heraldic fabulous beast primarily represented as rampant horned lion with an armed human rider on the back and a warrior counter player attacking it from behind. Usually depicted in the recesses of the jaṅghā.
Śikhara	Literally meaning head, the term stands for the principal spire or tower over the sanctum or garbhagriha. A tall curvilinear śikhara capped by an āmalaka and kalaśa is the most distinctive feature of the Northern temple style.
Śriṅga	Miniature śikhara.
Staṁbha	Pillar, shaft of the pillar.
Staṁbha-sakha	A sakha of the doorway representing a pilaster.

Sukanāsika	Pediment shaped roof over the antarāla. The sukanāsika is a prominent feature of the front elevation of a developed Northern temple and must be higher than the pinnacle of the maṇḍapa roof.
Stupi or Stupikā	South Indian term for the finial of a temple.
Udgama	Pediment of Caitya arches crowning a niche.
Upana	South Indian term for the lowest moulding of adhiṣṭhāna.
Ura-mañjarī	Smaller replica of the main śikhara addorsed to the central ratha of the śikhara.
Ura-śriṅga	Same as Ura-mañjarī.
Vījapūraka	Citrus fruit design represented above the kalaśa, stopper forming the terminal decoration of the śikhara.
Vimāna	South Indian term used for the entire towered sanctuary from the base to the finial.
Vyāla	Śāradūla.
Yoni-paṭṭa	Base or receptacle of Śiva-Liṅga, also called pīṭha, pīṭhika or Gauri-paṭṭa.

PLAN AND PLATES

Pl.1. Side View of Kandariya Mahadeva Temple

Pl.2. Close View of Kandariya Mahadeva Temple

Pl.3. Erotic Kama Sculpture of Kandariya Mahadeva Temple, Khajuraho India

Pl.4. Sculpture at Kandariya Mahadeva Temple

Pl.5. Shiva and Parvati share an easy familiarity, as depicted in this famous sculpture at Khajuraho.

Pl.6. The Craftsmen of Khajuraho created figures that were voluptuously graceful. Here, a beautiful young woman fastens an anklet on her foot, helped by an attendant.

Pl.7. Some of the individual sculpture at Khajuraho.
A sardula or mythical animal sculpture.

Pl.8. Various Sculpture at Kandariya Mahadeva Temple.

Pl.12. Full View of Kandariya Mahadeva Temple, Khajuraho

Pl.11. Animal sculpture at Kandariya Mahadeva Temple, Khajuraho

Pl.10. Erotic Sculpture at Kandariya Mahadeva Temple, Khajuraho

Pl.9. Amorous Couple on North Wall of Kandariya Mahadeva Temple, Khajuraho

Pl.13. Sculpture at Kandariya Mahadeva Temple, Khajuraho

Pl.14. Animal Sculpture at Kandariya Mahadeva Temple, Khajuraho

Pl.15. Close View of Sculpture at Kandariya Mahadeva Temple, Khajuraho

Pl.16. Details of Sculptures at Kandariya Mahadeva Temple, Khajuraho